Dump Trucks

Aaron Frisch

CREATIVE EDUCATION

Published by Creative Education
P.O. Box 227, Mankato, Minnesota 56002
Creative Education is an imprint of
The Creative Company
www.thecreativecompany.us

Design by Ellen Huber
Production by Chelsey Luther
Art direction by Rita Marshall
Printed in the United States of America

Photographs by Dreamstime (Artzzz, John Casey, Tomo
Jesenicnik, Dmitry Kalinovsky, Kuzma, Sergey Milovidov,
Upthebanner), Getty Images (Lester Lefkowitz), iStockphoto
(Jerry McElroy), Shutterstock (Baloncici, Robert J. Beyers II,
max blain, dgmata, ericlefrancais, fckncg, Zacarias Pereira
da Mata, Pi-Lens, TFoxFoto, Alaettin YILDIRIM)

Library of Congress Cataloging-in-Publication Data
Frisch, Aaron.
Dump Trucks / Aaron Frisch.
p. cm. — (Seedlings)
Summary: A kindergarten-level introduction to dump
trucks, covering their size, movement, role in the process of
construction, and such defining features as their beds and
large wheels.
Includes bibliographical references and index.
ISBN 978-1-60818-341-8
1. Dump trucks—Juvenile literature. I. Title.

TL230.F75 2013
629.225—dc23   2012023422

9 8 7 6 5 4

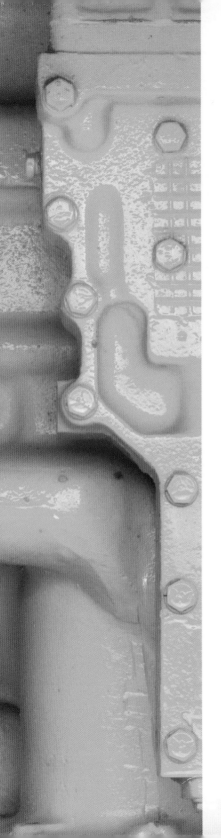
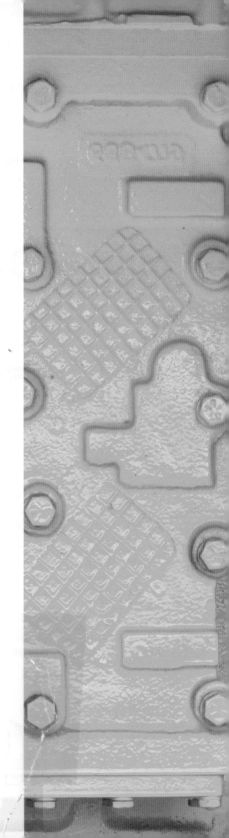

TABLE OF CONTENTS

Time to dump!

Dump trucks are big trucks.

They carry all kinds of loads.

A dump truck has a big bed. The bed lifts up. This dumps the load out.

A dump truck has big wheels.

The wheels help the truck carry heavy loads over bumpy ground.

Dump trucks carry dirt and rocks. They carry trash and rubble, too.

Most dump trucks are big. Some dump trucks are bigger than houses!

Machines like diggers put things in dump trucks. The trucks carry the load away.

Then they dump it.

17

All done dumping!

Picture a Dump Truck

rock shield

cab

hood

bumper

load

bed

wheel

Words to Know

bed: the part of a truck used to carry things

diggers: machines that dig holes and pick up dirt

rubble: pieces of broken buildings

Read More

Gardner, Charlie, ed. *See How They Go: Trucks.*
New York: DK Publishing, 2009.

Sobel, June. *B Is for Bulldozer: A Construction ABC.*
San Diego: Gulliver Books, 2003.

Websites

Big Trucks for Kids
http://www.bigtrucksforkids.com/dump-truck-videos.html
This site has pictures and videos of dump trucks at work.

Free Construction Coloring Pages
http://www.squidoo.com/free-construction-coloring-pages
This site has dump truck pictures. You can print and color them.

Index